BUSINESS LAW PART 2: THE SALE OF GOODS ACT, 1930

A SIMPLIFIED VERSION OF THE SALE OF GOODS ACT

M VASANTHA

Made with ♥ on the Notion Press Platform
www.notionpress.com

I would like to dedicate this book to my sister Mrs.Karuna, my dad Mr.Venkateswararao and my mom Mrs.Nagalskshmi.

Contents

Preface

As a student with no law base studying business law as a subject at the university was hard, even the text books availabe were hard to understand and they had very few illustrtations, but then trying to link the law concepts to things around me made it easier to remeber and undersatnd the concepts better.

The main reason for me to write this, is to help the students studying business law understand the concepts in a better manner using illustrations and examples that they can relate to, relatability of the concepts is extremely important for students to understand and retain the concepts that they study.

Acknowledgements

I would like to dedicate this book to my sister Mrs.Karuna, my dad Mr.Venkateswararao and my mom Mrs.Nagalskshmi. Secondly, my friends who have supported me all through the process of writing this book.

Specially, I would like to thank Ms.Garapatai Gouri Sathvika Chowdary and Mr.Anirudh Devarakonda for constantly reading and giving a feedback to my work, without their constant support this book wouldn't have seen light of the day.

CHAPTER ONE

INTRODUCTION TO BUSINESS LAW

Why is it Necessary to understand the law?

Having the knowledge of the law is essential because breaking the law cannot be justified by ignorance. In Latin "Ignorantia legis non excusat" which translates to ignorance of the law is not an excuse and, in this context, ignorance is not knowing the law.

Law, in general, is divided into several parts

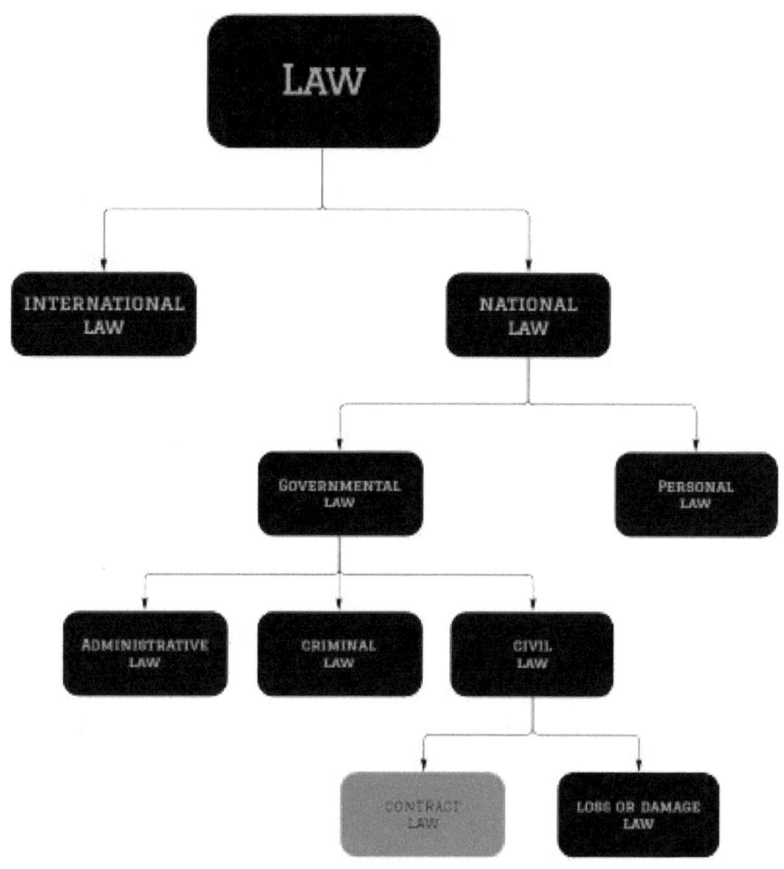

Types of Law

The whole set of Business Law is known as "*Mercantile law*"

In this part, we mainly focus on Sale of goods act, 1930.

Why is it important to understand Sale of goods act in general?

Every person who buys/ uses any goods that are put out for public is a part of sale, and as a party to sales it is necessary to know all the rights and essentials of a sale process.

The Indian contract is essentially divided in 3 parts, I from section 1-75 which deals with the general principles of contract act, *the second part section 76-123 contained principles related to sales, which is now a part of The Sale of goods act, 1930,* the third part i.e., from section 124-238 deals with certain special kinds of contracts.

The contracts of sale or nay case related to sale of goods made before 1930 will come under The Indian contract act, 1872, and the ones made in or after 1930 will be considered under the Sale of goods act, 1930. Sale of goods act is complementary to Indian contact act.

The sale of goods act came into effect on the 1st of July, 1930; and it extends to the whole of India including Jammu and Kashmir which were previously not included.

The provisions of the act are applicable to the contracts related to the sale of goods (movable properties and not immovable properties).

CHAPTER TWO

INTERPRETATION CLAUSE

Short title - This Act may be called the sale of goods act, 1930.

Extent & commencement - The act applies to the whole of India including Jammu and Kashmir and it came into effect on the 1st of July, 1930.

**Interpretation clause: expressly explains the parties' intent for specific grammatical rules to be construed **

Interpretation clause for the Sale of goods act, 1930

"According to section 2[1(a)], "action" includes counterclaim and set-off"

"According to section 2[1(b)], "buyer" means a person who buys or agrees to buy goods;"

"According to section 2[1(c)], "contract of sale" includes an agreement to sell as well as the sale;"

"According to section 2[1(d)], "delivery" means voluntary transfer of possession from one person to another;"

"According to section 2[1(e)], "document of title to goods" has the same meaning as it has in The Factors Act;"

"According to section 2[1(f)], "fault" means a wrongful act or default;"

"According to section 2[1(g)], "future goods" means goods to be manufactured or acquired by the seller after the making of the contract of sale;"

"According to section 2[1(h)], "goods" includes all chattels personal other than things in action or money and includes emblements, industrial growing crops and things attached to or forming part of the land which are agreed to be severed before sale or under the contract of sale;"

"According to section 2[1(i)], "property" means the general property in goods and not merely a special property;"

"According to section 2[1(j)], "quality of goods" includes their state or condition;"

"According to section 2[1(k)], "sale" includes a bargain and sale as well as a sale and delivery;"

"According to section 2[1(l)], "seller" means a person who sells or agrees to sell goods;"

"According to section 2[1(m)], "specific goods" means goods identified and agreed upon at the time a contract of sale is made;"

"According to section 2[1(n)], "warranty" means an agreement with reference to goods that are the subject of a contract of sale but collateral to the main purpose of the contract, the breach of which gives rise to a claim for damages but not to a right to reject the goods and treat the contract as repudiated."

"According to section 2[2], A thing is deemed to be done "in good faith" within the meaning of this Act when it is in fact done honestly whether it be done negligently or not."

"According to section 2[3], A person is deemed to be insolvent within the meaning of this Act who either has ceased to pay his debts in the ordinary course of business or cannot pay his debts as they become due."

"According to section 2[4], Goods are in a "deliverable state" within the meaning of this Act when they are in such a state that the buyer would under the contract be bound to take delivery of them."

CHAPTER THREE

FORMATION OF CONTRACT OF SALE

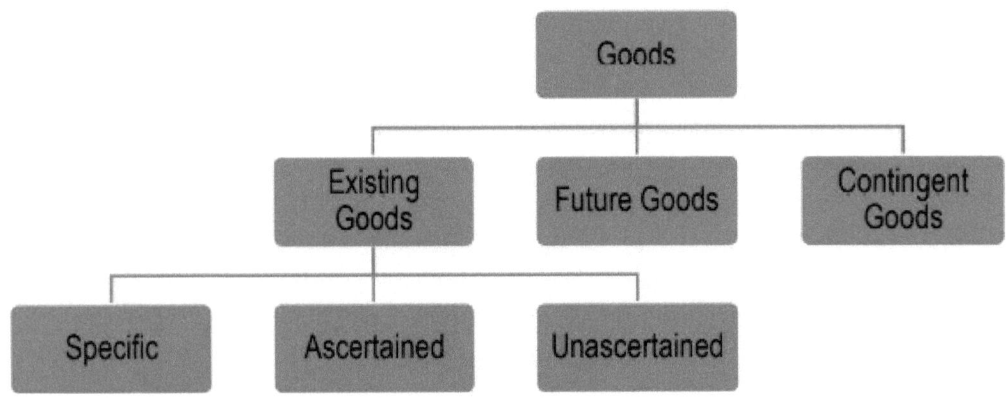

Types of goods

Since this law deals with the sale of (Tangible) goods, it is necessary to know the different types of goods.

The good types are as follows:

1. Existing goods: As the name suggests, existing goods are those that, at the time of the Sales Agreement, Seller owns or possesses the Goods offered for sale as referred to in Section 6.
example: Sujay owns a MacBook Pro and offers it for sale. In this case, the MacBook Pro is considered a pre-existing good because Sujay has title and/or possession of the good offered for sale.

A. Specific Goods: They are the goods identified and agreed upon at the time the purchase contract was formed, as per Section 2 (14).

example: Venkat has five phones of different brands in his collection and he agreed to sell his Samsung Galaxy S23 and Karuna agreed to buy the same phone. In this case, the Samsung Galaxy S23 is considered a specific good.

B. Ascertained goods: These are goods marked as agreed after conclusion of the purchase contract.
example: Sathvika goes to Sangeetha taai's shop and from a pile of 50 apples she picks 10 apples. The 10 apples she picked and set aside are called ascertained goods, because the commodities to be purchased are determined.

2. Future Commodities: These are goods that the Seller is required to manufacture, produce or acquire even after the contract for ownership has been entered into as per Section 2(6).
example: Anirudh goes to Gangaram's canteen and buys a Chole Bhature, but the Bhature has not yet been made. In this case Bhature is a future commodity as the seller has not yet manufactured it.

3.Contingent Goods:
These are goods for which the contract for the purchase of goods is dependent on another uncertain event as per Article 6(2).
example: I agree to sell the book on Contract act provided that it is published by penguin house publication. Now, whether or not I agree to sell my book on depends on whether or not Penguin House Publications will publish my book.

A sales contract is concluded only when title and ownership of the goods are transferred to the offeree/promisor. Delivery therefore plays an important role in the contract of sale of goods.

Therefore, it is necessary to know the different types of shipping.
Delivery: Delivery is the voluntary transfer of ownership from one person to another in accordance with section 2 paragraph 2.
Various forms of delivery are shown below.

1. Actual delivery:
Actual delivery of the goods occurs upon receipt of physical possession of the goods offered for sale.
example: Haripriya purchased a watch from Myntra and the watch was delivered to him within a week. In this case the delivery of the watch will be counted as the actual delivery.

2. Constructive delivery: If done without changing custody or actual ownership of the item, such as service by receipt.
example: Abhai, a vegetable dealer, sells the onions to Mr. Patchipulusu and asks Barry to keep the onions on behalf of Patchipulusu. In this case, when Barry confirms that he is holding the item on his behalf, the delivery is said to be a constructive delivery.

3. Symbolic delivery: Where there is a delivery of a thing in token of transfer of something else.
example: Haripriya brought a Bentley car and instead of the actual good (car) being delivered the key is delivered to her, in this case the key is a symbolic representation of the car and this process is called symbolic delivery.

CHAPTER FOUR

FORMATION OF THE CONTRACT

CONTRACT OF SALE OF GOODS

According to Article 4 of sale of goods act, a contract for the sale of goods is a contract in which the seller transfers, or agrees to transfer, the ownership of the goods to the buyer in exchange for consideration (price).

ESSENTIALS OF A CONTRACT OF SALE OF GOODS:

1. Bilateral contract: A contract for the sale of goods must be a two-way contract (Bilateral), as the goods are intended to be transferred from one person to another.
2. Transfer of property: The purpose of the contract for the sale of goods must be the transfer of title/ownership of the goods from one person to another.
3. Goods: The subject of the contract must be the product.
4. Price or money consideration: Any exchange of goods must be for consideration (price or money) and not exchange for other goods.
5. Essential elements of a valid contract: In general, a contract for the sale of goods should contain all the elements of a valid

Well, essentially many people tend to confuse the agreement to sell and actual sale, and hence it is extremely essential for one to know the distinction between sale and a mere agreement to sell.

As per section 4 (1) – "A contract of sale of goods is a contract whereby the seller transfers or agrees to transfer the property in goods to the buyer for a price. There may be a contract of sale between one part-owner and another."

As per section 4 (2) – "A contract of sale may be absolute or conditional."

As per section 4 (3) – "Where under a contract of sale the property in the goods is transferred from the seller to the buyer, the contract is called a sale, but where the transfer of the property in the goods is to take place at a future time or subject to some condition thereafter to be fulfilled, the contract is called an agreement to sell."

As per section 4 (4) – "An agreement to, sell becomes a sale when the time elapses or the conditions are fulfilled subject to which the property in the goods is to be transferred."

An agreement to sell is a mere agreement and it is yet to be performed but a sale is when the good is actually sold and the performance by all the parties to contract is completed.

The following points will give a better overview of the distinction between a sale and an agreement to sell:

1. In sale the possession and ownership of the goods is passed to the buyer at the time of the contract who then becomes the owner of the good(s)
   Whereas
   In an agreement to sell the ownership or the possession of the goods is not transferred to the buyer at the time of the contract, it only passes when the performance of all the parties to contract is completed.
2. A sale is a contract that is executed
   Whereas
   an agreement to sell is a contract that is yet to be performed or an executory contract.

3. Sale is a contract along with transporting the good
   whereas
   an agreement to sell is a mere simple contract without the transportation.
4. In a sale if the goods are destroyed by accident the liability will fall on the buyer as, in a sale the buyer immediately becomes the owner of the goods.
   Whereas
   in an agreement to sell if the goods are destroyed by accident the liability falls upon the seller as the ownership is not transferred yet.
5. If there is an agreement to sell and the seller commits a breach, the buyer has only a personal remedy against the seller, namely, a claim for damages.
   Whereas
   if there has been a sale, and the seller commits a breach by refusing to deliver the goods, the buyer has not only a personal remedy against him but also the other remedies which an owner has in respect of goods themselves such as a suit for conversion or detenue.

Yet gain there is another concept that is generally confused with sale: Bailment, therefore it is necessary for one to know the difference between Sale and bailment.

Sale is a mere executed contract wherein a transfer of ownership in exchange for a price paid.
whereas
Bailment is the delivery of goods to a person from another, where it may or may not involve price, where the good delivered returned disposed off as mentioned in the contract.

Example: Karuna took Vasantha's cycle for a ride with her permission and karuna has to return Vasantha's cycle to her after the use.

Example: Kamya gave her earphones to Abhai and they while making the contract Kamya has told Abhai that after his use he can dispose it off by selling it off and this disposal can be done if and only if the parties to the contract have previously agreed upon disposing the good.

The most important point is that there is no intention of the transfer of goods ownership and there is no actual transfer of property.

As per section 7 of the sale of goods act: when there is a contract for the sale of specific goods and the goods are perished before making the contract without the knowledge of the seller have perished or damaged the seller is no longer liable to meet the terms of the contract.

As per section 8 of the sale of goods act: when there is an agreement to sell specific goods and the goods perish or become without any fault on the seller or buyer's part the contract need not be executed and can be avoided.

Modes of fixing price

As per section 9(1) of sale of goods act the price of the good being sold may be predetermined or be left to be determined in due course in the manner agreed upon, or be determined at a future point of time by the course of dealing between the parties.

Example: Mr. Aarav and Mr. Gunther made an agreement of sale wherein Mr. Gunther the seller will sell his Harley Davidson bike, in such a case the exact price may be pre-determined at the time of making a contract or can be decided upon at a later period of time.

As per section 9(2) in a situation where the price is not determined in any of the ways as mentioned in section 9(1) the buyer shall pay a reasonable price, and the reasonable price will be determined as per the facts of the case and can change from case to case.

Example: In the abovementioned example the price is not set and is not set before the delivery by Mr.Gunther then Mr.Aarav must pay a reasonable amount say 5lakhs in this case as Harley Davidson is a luxury bike, the reasonable price is different for different cases

As per section 10(1) in a situation where the price is to be determined by the valuation of a third party and in case such third party cannot or doesn't determine the price the agreement need not be executed and hence can be avoided.

Example: If in the above mentioned example Mr.Aarav and Mr.Gunther decided to get in a second hand bike valuer Ms.Kerah to determine the price of the bike and Ms.Kerah dies and hence the values of the bike cant be determined then the agreement need not be executed.

As per section 10(2) in a situation where the third party that is to determine the price, is prevented from doing so at the fault of the seller or buyer, the party that is not at fault may file a suit against the party at fault.

Example: If in the above mentioned example Mr.Aarav and Mr.Gunther decided to get in a second hand bike valuer Ms.Kerah to determine the price of the bike and Ms.Kerah is restricted by Mr.Gunther and because of that Ms.Kerah is not able to determine the price of the bike then Mr.Aarav is in a position to file a suit against Mr.Gunther as because of him the agreement is not being executed.

CONDITIONS AND WARRANTIES:

As per section 11 Unless otherwise stated in the terms and conditions, payment terms shall not be considered an integral part of the purchase agreement. Whether a separate time determination is essential to the contract depends on the terms of the contract.

As per section 12(1) “A stipulation in a contract of sale with reference to goods which are the subject thereof may be a condition or a warranty.”

As per section 12(2) a condition is a requirement to fulfill the purpose of the contract and breaching a condition would result in the repudiation (rejection) of the contract.

As per section 12(3) a warranty is a requirement term to a contract and breaching a warranty would not result in the repudiation (rejection) of the contract.

As per section 12(4) at times, whether the requirement of a sale is a condition or warranty depends on the case and at times a requirement to fulfill the contract maybe be a condition though it is called a warranty in the contract.

When can a condition be called a warranty?

As per section 13(1) (2) (3) in the following cases a condition can be treated as a warranty.

1. If the contract of sale is subject to conditions met by the seller, the buyer may waive the condition or treat any breach of the condition as a breach of warranty and not as a basis for treating the contract as circumvention.
2. If the contract of sale is integral and the buyer accepts the goods or any part thereof, any breach of the conditions to be performed by the seller can only be treated as a breach of warranty. Refusal to accept the goods shall not be grounds for terminating the contract, unless there is a time limit. For this purpose, we enter into contracts, express or implied.
3. The contents of this section shall not affect the performance of conditions or warranties. Impossible or otherwise legally exempt.

Implied Warranties [Section 14(b), 14(c) and 16(3)]

a. In the case of a sale, an implied condition on the part of the seller that they have the right to sell
   In the case of goods and sales contracts, the right to sell the goods at the time
   when handing over the property.
b. An implied warranty that the purchaser will have and enjoy goods uninterrupted;
c. Implied warranties that the goods will not be charged benefit to third parties that are not stated or informed by the buyer before or on the conclusion of the contract.

Implied conditions under a sale by description

1. Goods must correspond with description: As per section 15 of the act when there is a sale as per the description of the goods, then there is an explicitly implied condition that the description of the good must match with the description given by the buyer.

2. Goods must also be merchantable quality: as per section 16(2) If you purchase the listed product from the seller who handles the listed product (regardless of whether he is the manufacturer or producer), if the goods are of sellable quality:
   If the purchaser inspects the goods, there are no implied conditions for defects that should have been revealed by such inspection.
   Merchantable quality: A reasonable person would consider the products to be of merchantable quality if they took current circumstances into consideration. If they have flaws that render them unfit for regular use or are such that a sane individual would not purchase them in light of those flaws, they are not marketable.
3. Condition as to wholesomeness: The provisions or eatables supplied must not only meet the description given but also, they must not have any defects and need to be wholesome or sound.
4. Condition as to quality or fitness for a particular purpose: There are usually no implied declarations in sales contracts. Any warranty or condition as to the quality or fitness of goods supplied for a particular purpose.
   However, there is an implied condition that the goods are reasonably fit for the purpose for which they are required if:
   (i) Buyer expressly or implicitly informs Seller of the particular purpose for which the goods are intended; they need to show that they rely on the skill and judgment of the seller.
   (ii) the goods conform to any description provided in the course of business of the seller (whether the seller is the producer or not). No such condition exists if the goods were purchased under a patent or tradename.
   Example: Ms. Tejaswini goes to the market to get raw mangoes that are fit for the purpose of making mango pickle and she doesn't know which kind of mangoes are fit and she expresses the same to the seller MS. Kaivalya and the seller gives Ms. Tejaswani raw mangoes that are not fit for making a pickle, in such a case to seller is liable to give Ms. Tejaswini the goods that are fit for the purpose for which they are required whether or not the mangoes are grown in Ms. Kaivalya's farm.

<u>Implied conditions under a sale by sample</u>

In a contract of sale by sample:

1. There is an implied condition that the quality of the bulk of the goods must match with the sample of the goods.
Example: Monica goes to Central Perk and asks Rachel for a sample of the muffin, and she orders 15 muffins to take with her and hence here there is an implied condition that the 15 muffins must match with the quality of the sample muffin.

2.The other implied condition is that the buyer shall compare the bulk with the sample given.
Example: Monica has all rights to compare the quality of the sample given to her with the 15 muffins that she has ordered.

3. There is an implied condition of the merchantability of the goods or hidden defects in the goods which may appear normal but may be not of the merchantability quality.
Example: The muffins delivered to Monica must not have any defects that are not visible on examination of the muffins. Its Rachel's responsibility to see to that the goods delivered to Monica are of merchantable quality.

CHAPTER FIVE

EFFECTS OF THE CONTRACT

Passing of Property or Transfer of Ownership:

As per section 18 Where it is a sales contract for unspecified products
Title to the goods is transferred to the purchaser until the goods are ascertained.

Example: If Chetan goes to the vegetable vendor and asks for a kilogram of onions, until and unless specifically 1kg of onions are set aside the title to the onions cant be transferred to him.

As per section 19(1) when a contract of sale of specific goods is made the property is transferred to the buyer at the time when the parties to the contract intend to.

Example: Anirudh made a contract of sale with Kamya for boat earbuds where they decided that the property will be transferred to Anirudh after 1 month.

As per section 19(2) The terms of the contract, the actions of the parties, and the circumstances of the case shall be used to determine the parties' decision.

As per section 19(3) Unless otherwise specified, the provisions of Sections 20 through 24 shall apply as provisions. The decision of the parties as to when title to the goods transfers to the buyer.

Passing of property in specific goods:

As per section 20 of the act when there is a contract made for the sale of specific goods that are in a deliverable state then the property in the goods is transferred to the buyer when the contract is made and the change in the time of delivery or the time of payment will not affect the passing of property in goods at once.

Example: Chetan made a contract with Karuna wherein karuna was to sell her book "IKIGAI" to Chetan for ?100, when this contract is made the property in goods is transferred to Chetan and this transfer of property, not dependent on the payment of the price or the time of delivery.

As per section 21 of the act when there is a contract of sale of specific goods but not in a deliverable state then the property in goods will not be transferred until the goods are put into a deliverable state.

Example: Chetan made a contract with Rolio digital wherein the vendor Rolio was to sell a PC (not assembled) to Chetan for ?50,000, when this contract is made the property in goods is not transferred to Chetan as the property is not in a deliverable state and the property in the goods will not be transferred until the good is in a deliverable state, in this case for the good to be of deliverable nature the PC needs to be assembled.

As per section 22 of the act when there is a contract made for the sale of specific goods in deliverable state but the seller needs to perform some act to ascertain the price of the good then the property in the goods would not be transferred until the price is ascertained and the same is conveyed to the buyer.

Example: Venkat wanted to buy a flat from Lakshmi and Lakshmi had no knowledge of the price of the fast as per the current market rate and hence to ascertain the price of the good Lakshmi hired a third party and the third party ascertained the price to be $45lakh and this information has to be conveyed to Venkat, until and unless the information is conveyed to Venkat the property in the goods will not be transferred.

As per section 24 of the act when goods are sent "on approval" or "on sale or return" or other terms similar to the abovementioned the property passes to the buyer under 2 conditions:

a. When the buyer signifies his acceptance to the seller or conveys his acceptance by doing some act adopting the transaction.

Example: Anirudh a dealer in pearl's sent a set of pearl jewellery to Sathvika the buyer on sale or return basis and Sathvika after observing the jewellery finds it nice and conveys her assent to Anirudh, in this case the goods will be transferred to the buyer.

b. If the buyer does not signify their acceptance and retains the goods with themselves without giving any notice for rejection, in such a case if the time fro the return of goods has been fixed, on the expiration of such time and if no time has been fixed then in such a case on the expiration of reasonable time.

Example: In the abovementioned example if Sathvika does not give acknowledgement for the jewellery the jewellery needs to be returned to Anirudh on the date specified if any, if not mentioned then on the expiry of reasonable time.

Passing of Risk:

As per section 26 unless otherwise mentioned the risk of the damage or destruction is with the seller until the property is transferred to the buyer and once the property is transferred to the buyer then risk is also transferred to the buyer, whether or not the delivery is made.

Example: Lakshmi entered into an agreement to sell some clothes to Karuna and in this case until the property is transferred to karuna Lakshmi will be liable for the risk and once the property is transferred to karuna, she will be solely liable for all the risk affixed with the goods.

Transfer of Title by Person not the Owner:

only the owner of the product can sell the product. Conversely, the sale of an item by a person who is not or is not authorized to own it does not confer title to the purchaser. Rules are expressed by the maxim "*Nemo Dat Quod Non Habet*" In other words, no one can transfer property that is not that they own. Therefore, even a bona fide buyer who purchases stolen goods from a thief, or from such a thief from an acquirer, has no right to the acquisition. You can't get effective rights because you can't give rights to anyone.

Example: Arima finds a ring of Barry and sells it to a third person who purchases it in exchange of consideration(price) in good faith, even though the third person bought the ring without the knowledge that Arima isn't the true owner of the ring, Barry has all the rights to recover it from the third person.

Exception to the General Rule:

1. Section 27 of the Sale of Goods Act 1930 deals with the sale of goods by a person who is not the owner of those goods. According to this section, if a person sells goods that he does not own, the buyer cannot acquire a better title than the seller had.
   Example: suppose Adhira sells a car to Bharath, but Adhira is not the owner of the car. In that case, Bharath will not acquire a better title than Adhira had. If the real owner of the car claims the car back from Bharath, Bharath cannot claim any rights over the car, even if he has paid the full price to Adhira.
   This means that a buyer should always ensure that the seller is the rightful owner of the goods before making the purchase. If the buyer fails to do so, he may face legal consequences, such as losing the goods or paying damages to the real owner.
2. Section 28 of the Sale of Goods Act 1930 deals with the sale by a person who is in possession of the goods after the sale. According to this section, if a person sells goods that he is in possession of after the sale, the buyer will receive a good title to the goods, even if the seller had no right to sell them, unless the buyer had knowledge of the seller's lack of authority to sell the goods.
   Example: Adhira sells a car to Bharath and delivers the possession of the car to Bharath. Later, A's creditor takes away the car from Adhira for non-payment of dues. In that case, B will still be the rightful owner of the car and can claim it back from Adhira 's creditor, unless Bharath had knowledge of Adhira 's lack of authority to sell the car.
   This means that if the seller is in possession of the goods after the sale, the buyer should ensure that the seller has the right to sell the goods. If the buyer fails to do so and the seller does not have the right to sell the goods, the buyer may lose the goods or may have to pay damages to the rightful owner.

3. Section 29 of the Sale of Goods Act 1930 deals with the sale of goods that are subject to a lien or charge. According to this section, if the goods are sold when they are subject to a lien or charge, the buyer will take the goods subject to that lien or charge, unless the buyer had no notice of the lien or charge at the time of the sale.
   Example: suppose Aayush sells a car to Banter, but the car is subject to a lien in favour of a bank. In that case, Banter will take the car subject to the lien, and the bank can repossess the car from Banter if Aayush fails to pay the loan. However, if Banter had no notice of the lien at the time of the sale, he may be able to claim damages from Aayush.
   This means that if the goods are subject to a lien or charge, the buyer should ensure that he has notice of the lien or charge before making the purchase. If the buyer fails to do so and the goods are subject to a lien or charge, he may lose the goods or may have to pay damages to the holder of the lien or charge.
4. Section 30 of the Sale of Goods Act 1930 deals with the sale of goods that are sold by a mercantile agent who has been given the goods under a valid authority. According to this section, if a mercantile agent sells goods that he has been given under a valid authority, the buyer will acquire a good title to the goods, even if the agent had no right to sell them, unless the buyer had notice of the agent's lack of authority to sell the goods.
   Example: Damini gives his car to Kara, who is a mercantile agent, for the purpose of selling it. Kara sells the car to Chad, who has no notice of any defect in Kara's authority to sell the car. In that case, Chad will acquire a good title to the car, even if Kara had no right to sell it.
   This means that if the goods are sold by a mercantile agent, the buyer should ensure that the agent has the right to sell the goods. If the buyer fails to do so and the agent does not have the right to sell the goods, the buyer may lose the goods or may have to pay damages to the rightful owner.

CHAPTER SIX

RIGHTS OF UNPAID SELLER AGAINST THE GOODS

Before you get to know the rights of an unpaid seller, you need to know who an unpaid seller is.

As per section 45 of the act "the seller of goods is deemed an unpaid seller within the meaning of the act when the whole of the price has not been paid or tendered or when a bill of exchange or other negotiable instrument has been received as a conditional payment and the condition on which it was received has not been fulfilled by reason of the dishonour of the instrument or otherwise."

The following are the rights of an unpaid seller as per section 46:

a. In case the property in the goods has been transferred to the buyer.

1. The unpaid seller has a right to retain the goods for the price while he is in possession of the goods.
2. In a case where the buyer turned insolvent the unpaid seller has a right to stop the goods that are in transit for delivery.
3. The unpaid seller has a right to resell the goods.

b. In case the property in goods has not been transferred to the buyer, the unpaid seller has a right to withhold the delivery similar and extending his rights of lien and stoppage in transit when the property has passed to the buyer.

As per section 47 an unpaid sellers lien is not extensive, and hence a seller can execute lien in the following cases

1. The unpaid seller who is in possession of the goods is entitled to retain the possession of the goods until tha payment of the price in the following cases

a. Where the goods have been sold without any stipulation as to credit;
b. Where the goods have been sold on credit but the term of credit has expired.
c. Where the buyer becomes insolvent

2. The seller may exercise his right of lien notwithstanding that he is in possession of the goods as agent or bailee for the buyer.

As per section 48 of the act when an unpaid seller has made part delivery of the goods, he may exercise his right of lien on the remainder part of the goods in possession of him.

Now there might be a question as to when this right of lien is terminated.

As per section 49 of the act the right of lien is terminated in the following cases

1. When he delivers the goods to a carrier or other bailee for the purpose of transmission to the buyer without reserving the right of disposal of the goods.
2. When the buyer or his agent lawfully obtains possession of the goods.

3. And finally, by waiver thereof

CHAPTER SEVEN

SUITS FOR BREACH OF CONTRACT

Though you got to know of what a contract for the sale of a good is, how to make it, the essentials , the effect of the contract, the performance and the rights reserved for an unpaid seller, you need to know of the remedies available for the breach of contract.

The following are the remedies available for the breach of a contract of sale:

1. As per section 55 of the act in case there a breach of a contract of sale wherein the property in goods has passed to the buyer then, the seller can sue the buyer for the amount (Suit for price).
   When under the contract the amount id payable on a certain day and the buyer neglects to do so the seller can sue the buyer for the amount even if the property is not transferred to the buyer.
2. As per section 56 of the act in a case where the buyer wrongfully refuses to pay for the goods the seller has a right to sue the buyer for the damages for non-acceptance.
3. As per section 57 of the act in a case where the seller wrongfully refuses to deliver the goods o the buyer, the buyer can sue the seller for the damages for non-delivery.
4. As per section 58 of the act in a case where the buyer or seller are not performing their respective parts, the aggrieved party can sue the other party for specific performance of the contract.

Section 59 of the act provides that:

(1) Where there is a breach of warranty by file seller, or where the buyer elects or is compelled to treat any breach of a condition on the part of the seller as a breach of warranty, the buyer is not by reason only of such breach of warranty entitled to reject the goods; but they may

(a) set up against the seller the breach of warranty in diminution or extinction of the price; or

(b) sue the seller for damages for breach of warranty.

(2) The fact that a buyer has set up a breach of warranty in diminution or extinction of the price does not prevent him from suing for the same breach of warranty if he has suffered further damage.

As per section 60 where either party rejects the contract before the date of delivery they may either treat the contract to be in force and wait till the date of delivery or may treat the contract as rejected and sue for the damages for the breach.

Section 61 of the act provides that:

(1) Nothing in this Act shall affect the right of the seller or the buyer to recover interest or special damages in any case where by law interest or special damages may be recoverable, or to recover the money paid where the consideration for the payment of it has failed.

(2) In the absence of a contract to the contrary, the Court may award interest at such rate as it thinks fit on the amount of the price

(a) to the seller in a suit by him for the amount of the price— from the date of the tender of the goods or from the date on which the price was payable;

(b) to the buyer in a suit by him for the refund of the price in a case of a breach of the contract on the part of the seller—from the date on which the payment was made.

References

Economic Business and Commercial Laws. (2022). ICSI; ICSI. https://www.icsi.edu/media/webmodules/Economic%20Business%20and%20Commercial%20Laws.pdf

Garg, R. (2022, October 28). The Sale of Goods Act, 1930. IPleaders. https://blog.ipleaders.in/the-sale-of-goods-act-1930/

Sale of Goods Act 1930. (n.d.). Retrieved March 7, 2023, from http://umeschandracollege.ac.in/pdf/study-material/busness-law/Sale%20of%20Goods%20Act%201930.pdf

Sale of Goods Act, 1930. (1930). Www.indiacode.nic.in. https://www.indiacode.nic.in/handle/123456789/2390?sam_handle=123456789/1362

Srivastava, S. (n.d.). B.com II Semester Subject-Business Law Topic-Sale of Goods Act 1930. https://www.lkouniv.ac.in/site/writereaddata/siteContent/202004061939435276sunita_com_sale_of_goods_act_1930.pdf

THE SALE OF GOODS ACT, 1930. (n.d.). Legislative.gov.in; legislative.gov.in. https://legislative.gov.in/sites/default/files/A1930-3_0.pdf

Printed by Libri Plureos GmbH in Hamburg, Germany